SOOTHING MASSAGE FOR THE MIND

VOLUME ONE

SOOTHING MASSAGE FOR THE MIND

DOUGLAS DODD

TABLE OF CONTENTS

DOUGLAS DODD

QUESTIONS[2]

Do you feel like anything?
Do you feel anything?
What can I do?
Do you know?
Can you tell me?
Can you help me?
Can I be helped?
Do I still have time?
Is time through with me?
Am I lost?
Will I ever be found?
Will I find you?
Do you really exist?
Should I go on?
Is there any reason?
Will I love again?
Do I need life?
Do I need you?
Do I need anyone?
Do I need anything?
Do I really need?
Can I stop?
Can I die?
When will I die?
Will I stop?
When it stops?
Will it stop?

Should I speak?
Can I see?
Is sadness mine?
Is happiness gone?
Will the Questions ever fade?

INTRODUCTION

Hi there, well, I got you started off with a poem to work your mind right away. It's called Questions² because I have another "Questions" poem (which will pop up later). I'll talk more about this poem in a few, but right now a few words from our sponsor.

I came up with the idea of this book because of a fellow co-worker of mine. Her name is Angie. At the time (late 2006), I had well over one hundred poems and I finally brought them to work. I let all of the girls read them (of course). This was a big step for me. I really hadn't let anyone read most of these poems, hell, not even my ex-wife.

Now at the time, my wife and I really weren't together and she was the cause of all my stress and depression, thus a lot of poems I did end up writing were because of the emotional roller coaster she put me through. The girls at work loved my poems among the other stories I let them read, but it was Angie that had said something that made my mind wonder. She said, "*I haven't read stuff this deep since 'Chicken Soup for the Soul'.*" She went on to say she needed a hot bubble bath and candles to read this stuff. Well, since I'm always thinking about writing something, I was like, "*Yeah, I can do that!*"

Then there it was.....The Project, that I thought was very feasible for me to do. The next step was actually doing it. First, I had to approach it. That's always something within itself when it comes to me wanting to write something. When I write a poem, it just flows out, but a story (short or long) more so the long ones, I have to see it through. I normally make an outline, yes that little thingy you all learned in school. I find doing that is very helpful to me and it keeps me organized and on track. Plus, I can see how I want the story or book to progress. Now that isn't to say that I can't change my mind, hell, I get better ideas everyday, but this way I have a clear idea. So, let me talk about this book, of course, that may be a little redundant statement for this book since I'll be talking throughout, but regardless I had a bunch of thoughts, and I needed to write them down. The first thing I felt I needed to do was come up with a book title. I feel that a title is everything. It's a little like a poem, it should give you an emotion after you read it, but a title has a lot more to it then just that. A title can do a few things for you, and you might even say one of these after reading a title:

1) Hmmm, That sounds interesting.
2) No, I don't think so.
3) Oh Yeah, That sounds good (sarcastic).
4) What? (scratching your head)

So now we have to see how my mind works, and if you understand... good, if not, that's okay. Anyway, I don't know how every author around the world chooses their titles, but this is one way I look at it. I know there can be many different ways to come up with a title, but I was looking at it as a sort of a spinoff of Chicken Soup. Now, I don't want to come off as a rip-off artist because I feel everything I do is original and that it has my spin. Plus, the fact that I have never read any Chicken Soup for the Soul book. I had to go to the bookstore to look at one, and to my amazement there was like 20 different ones and I was like, "Shit, fuck me!" I also noticed that none of the books are by just one author. Then it came to me….maybe I could make a book with the potential of becoming a series.

As my mind was in it's little world, I thought to myself, "I need a great title for this book." I wanted something that was catchy, but similar and different at the same time. So, I was on one of my many walks during the Witching Hour and I was telling myself…..."Okay, Doug, you can't use CHICKEN SOUP, or any other food really." I needed to come up with something that was going to be Key for my series of books. So I was there very late at night thinking, "what is relaxing?," and "what does everyone in the world have that needs to be put to ease from time to time?"

Then I had it, Massage and Mind. Massage because I've been told that I give great ones, and my Mind is what I'm trying to put at ease. Next, I needed to put it into a short, simple and smooth sentence. *Soothing Massage for the MIND*. I was happy and I felt that I could write the perfect book. There you have it, so let's get this Soothing   Massage   going.

The Path

He walks out of his house to take a little walk to a love's house. The day is beautiful. Clear skies. Birds chirping. A light breeze. A day that could only bring smiles. His love's house is, but only a mile away.

He starts his walk with great energy and spirit. He walks down the dirt road that seems to go on forever with the tall trees hugging it all the way. He takes his time to notice the little animals in the forest. Squirrels chasing after each other. Foxes play fighting. He thinks to himself, "What a fairytale."

He walks for over an hour and thinks, "I should just about be there." He looks down the path, and as before, it goes on forever.

He walks for another hour, and still hasn't reached his love's house. He looks down the path again, and it seems as if he never left his house. Even with this view, and how long he has walked, his smile stays on.

He walks and walks and walks some more. The afternoon becomes early evening. The sky fills with clouds. The breeze becomes deathly cold. The birds stop singing. The squirrels have all gone home. The foxes' playfulness has turned into evil stares and growls. The path still goes on forever.

For some reason, he knows that this love was a dream. He stops his journey. He turns around to go home.............. and his smile still stays on.

1

I was wondering how I should start this book out and then it came to me on one of my many walks I like to take at night. The Path was a little something I wrote long ago, but thought it would be a nice pug in the beginning of this book.   The Path's intentions were that, you may have a lot of things on your mind, but don't forget to smile if you forget something or miss out on something. I was thinking I should set the guidelines for *Soothing Massage for the Mind*: 1) If you like, just take in a little at a time. 2) All that I'm offering are suggestions.

PLEASE!!! I don't feel that anyone should be told what they should do, or how they should live their life. Everyone is special. Every special individual handles situations in different ways. Then why would some individuals feel the need to tell whomever how they should be. So what I have done here….with the tangled web, I call my mind, is to set forth a journey for the mind of readers willing to take a chance.

I realize that most of this book will be poems (all written by me of course ☺) and just a little bit of commentary from me. I felt that a poetry book might just be too plain and since I was making this my first collection of poems…..well…..I wanted to add a little flare to it. I know, I could have just added pictures. Sorry…I can't draw.

I am putting a lot of personal poems in here and I feel that talking about life can help. For instance, the first poem that I started with on here Questions[2] is something many of us do. One thing that any human being can do, is Question everything. Of course, throughout the ages, many people got killed for doing that such thing, but isn't that better than just keeping your mouth shut and holding everything in? I'm not the sheep kind of person, and I like to say what's on my mind. I do hold my tongue at times, but that's generally when I know it wouldn't do any good anyway. So, please…don't ask me any stupid questions, okay? LOL These poems are straight from my crazy mind and everything else I have to put in there.

So, let's get back to what I was saying about suggestions and not being told what to do. I feel that everyone should be given the tools or choices. Life is a trial and some people never get it right. I think if you have the time and the energy, you should gather as much information you can and do some trial and error. Sometimes you never know what works best for you, until you try it.

2

Patience is a virtue. That's a statement that has been passed down from the ages. Of course, when you're a kid and hear this, you're like…. "Then WHY do I have to wait so long?" It seems funny, but at the same time, it's a bit sad because all of a sudden time passes you by and you're like,…."Where did it go?" So, let's share a poem about time.

WAITING FOR TIME

Waiting for Time?
To do What?
To find a Solution?
A Solution for What?

Happiness?
Sadness?
Love?
Hate?

Does the Means,
Equal the End?
Are we always Lost?
Even from the Start?

Knowing how to Start,
Lost in the Shuffle,
The End not Seen,
Or just an Illusion?

Are my eyes Open?
Or really Closed?
Don't forget to Breathe,
Waiting for Time.

3

This is one of my poems about procrastination. Pretty much, don't let Time get the best of you. Don't get lost in Time. Remember that you're not the one waiting on Time, but can you catch up? I do have quite a few poems on Time, but I wanted to share one more with you that's a play on words.

YESTERDAY, TODAY, AND TOMORROW

Yesterday is the day that you wish,
You could change Tomorrow,
Yesterday is the day of your past sorrow.

Today is Yesterday's Tomorrow,
As Today is Tomorrow's Yesterday,
Today is the day that you try to change,
To make Tomorrow a better day.

Tomorrow is the next day after Today,
Tomorrow is the day that you realize,
You didn't do anything Yesterday to change Today.

So remember, that Yesterday is the past,
You can't change,
But Today is the day you can change,
And when you do so,
Tomorrow wouldn't be the Today that is thinking
about Yesterday.

I love to write and that is an understatement. I write whenever I get a chance and sometimes when I get a chance and I don't have anything to write about….I get MAD. Now what is that good for? Do I write a poem about that? Now I do have a few poems about that and as I started to write them I got or I should say FOUND inspiration. Now this may sound a little funny, and here it goes. I can find inspiration in anything, but sometimes I'm like, "Naw, I just feel like touching on this subject today." Or I would put something off. I know, why would I just put it off? Sometimes I feel that I know if I start to write about something that is going to take forever to write, I'm like, "Okay, How much time do I have right now and do I feel like finishing this up later?" Generally, I fuck myself because I put it off for later feeling that I need to devote more time to it, and that's when I totally forget about it. I would have to say that the pain in the ass about it is that this happens to me all the time. I do get mad and upset when I forget to write down an idea, but I soon let it pass because I have ideas everyday, hundreds upon hundreds that I haven't gotten to and I hope I can get to them in this lifetime.

4

Sometimes I feel that I'm too passive. Then, I think, I'm never satisfied. Of course, that's not totally true, I do have my joys in life and wonder if those are enough? I may let too many things go and at the same time I'll hold certain things (whether it's words or actions) too close to my heart that continually hurt me. Now WHY would I do something like this? I feel that everyone does this whether they show the hurt or seem to be as perfect as possible. The brain is like a computer (not like you haven't heard that one before) and this makes me think of a good movie(I know…a book, too) that shows this very well is….Dreamcatcher. I just loved how the guy had different floors and files inside his head. I really loved that. Now most people don't have control like he did in the movie. We need a catalyst , maybe a smell, maybe a street corner, or maybe a certain song and when something like that happens, we generally go, "Damn, I almost forgot about that."

CAN'T TURN IT OFF

Can't Turn It Off,
Sour Thought,
After Sour Thought,
Nothing but Bad Taste.

Where's the new breeze?
A Fresh Thought,
A Sweet Thought,
No Refreshing Drink.

Still Looking for a Change,
Still Searching for My Soul,
Still Fighting,
Still Losing.

Still Can't Turn It Off,
Walk a Million miles,
To savor a Thought,
For my own bitterness.

Where's that sugar mound?
I just want to lay down,
Enjoy the Taste in my mouth,
Dream a little Dream.

Still Can't Turn It Off,
A burden in my hands,
The weight on my shoulders,
A Journey I Must Take.

I bet you are wondering why I chose this one, huh? Well, probably not, but I'm gonna tell you anyway. Now, I could tell you the real reason behind this poem, but I don't have to, to give you a great reason behind the poem. Writing is a great way to release anything that's on your mind or any emotion you're having. The beauty of *Can't Turn It Off* is that it's the fuel that fills a writer. At least there is no worry of writer's block. I normally don't get writer's block, even though I have a couple poems about it, as much as the need is to make everything perfect.

Can't Turn It Off doesn't have to be for just writers, but anyone with a lot on their mind. The thing I tried to do in the last couple verses was to have the person be hopeful in that this burden can be shifted to something happy and just embrace the burden until then. So here's another poem along the lines of *Can't Turn It Off.*

PEACE AND BALANCE

Where is that peace of mind?
Is it in the music?
Is it in the burning aroma?
Is it in the Love?

Where can that balance be found?
Is it deep within Me?
Is it in the great beyond?
Is it just a dream?

Thought upon Thought,
Poem upon Poem,
As I thread another needle,
As I walk another mile,
Where will I be?
Thoughtless and alone?
Old and tired?
Enlightened and Saved?

I would hope for the latter.
Life is too short,
Not to have that,
Peace and Balance.

5

How important is Life? I would assume that this is a very important question. Now when you ask a question like this, there will be other little questions to follow, that may need to be answered first. Then we can get to the main question at hand.

What do I measure that equals my life's worth?
My Morals? What are My Morals?
My Life? Is Money My Life?
Is Family My Life? Is Work My Life?

Well, there could be a million other questions, but I don't measure things the same as a million other people, so this is a question for you all to have fun with. Now the real reason for asking this question is because it's a question you can ask anyone or ask about any situation on any day. One point I would like to touch on is cell phones. How important is Life? You can't use a cell phone at work. How important is Life? You can't use a cell phone while driving. How important is Life? For Restrictions? For your Safety? It's Our Policy? I'm really against limitations and in America there are far too many. Of course, I would like to quote Dirty Harry, "Man has to know his limitations." I love that statement and I think it is so true. BUT… I feel that everyone should find those limits on their own and not be told where they have to stop. For example that would be like if you or if you know someone that feels uncomfortable driving while talking on the phone. They have found out that is a limitation of theirs. No driving and talking on the cell.

Now I'm not going to ramble on and on and bitch about everything I can't stand. I do think that it is good to vent and because of that I plan on writing another book, whether this one is a hit or not. I will just say this….this other book will be LOUD. I'm just letting you know I'm one sarcastic MF and when I vent I try to turn it into a joke or I just sound like a crazed raving mad lunatic and everyone just laughs at me. Hey, that's fine, at least I feel better.

Now, I wouldn't advise you to all of a sudden change into a smart-ass overnight if that isn't you. That's why I asked that question. How Important is Life? What is Important to You? What makes You, You? Maybe....What Matters?

THE MATTER

Does it Matter?
What really Matters?
Is it that cup of joe?
Is it just to wake up?

What if it isn't anything at all?
Can you deal with it?
Do you just put it away?
Do you save it for yourself?

Can you really say what it is?
I like to say it's Love,
But that's like a can of soda,
It's good as long as it lasts.

I could say it's Life,
And I would be right,
But that would be too vague,
And just a guideline for the topic at hand.

So what really does Matter?
It's different for you,
Different for me,
Different from day to day.

I just won't judge your choice,
If you don't judge mine,
Remember to have no regret,
Always make it Matter.

What does Matter? What is the Matter that we are talking about? This is for me to figure out not for you.   I wrote this because I was in one of those kind of moods. What does Matter? Sometimes, you can never find the answer and will forever ask that question. Sometimes, you'll know what it is, but will never find it. Sometimes, there are the lucky ones that truly get it. Sometimes, what Matters, changes throughout your life. Just try to remember everything you do, make it Matter.

6

For some reason, I don't write too much at home. I mean, yeah, I do, but for some reason I would much rather go somewhere and write. Maybe it's the scenery I like. Maybe it's the people watching I like to do. Maybe it's just to be out. Maybe one day I'll find that special place where all my creative juices flow. I hope it doesn't take my whole lifetime….that would suck. I think far too many people aren't happy where they are. Now, I'm not just talking about jobs. I don't think they are living where they want. Now, I know it isn't as easy as changing a roll of toilet paper. The biggest factor is money. The Root of all Evil. Now, I don't need to talk about how money makes the world go around, but how it may get in the way of happiness. I know….you shouldn't need money to find LOVE or HAPPINESS, but living in America….it sure would seem like that. I wish I could change things, but I can't. I wish I could change a lot of things, but hey…that's entirely another book. Some people really allow their lives to pass them by. One movie really good at showing this is "CLICK". I'm sure everyone at some point in their life has felt this "Where has the time gone?" feeling. I think when it gets to this point, where you seem to be asking yourself that question a lot, it just may be time to do something. *Soothing Massage for the Mind* has become that step for me. On the verge of turning 30 years old and a failed marriage, I needed to step forward. Of course, it's a state of mind, and getting to that level of moving on can be very hard. The funny thing is, and I probably can't stress this enough, is the importance of movies, music and books. It could be something sung, written, or shown that gives you strength or the will to carry on. Those simple reminders. I say that just because as I write about something, I sometimes get hit with those simple reminders. This always gives you a greater appreciation. This in return may help you find that path along your long journey.   Sometimes you just have to listen.

JUST LISTEN

Just listen to the Silence,
Peaceful,
Serene,
Mysterious.

Listen to the Wind,
Gentle,
Smooth,
Whispering.

Listen to the Ocean,
Rolling,
Swishing,
Crashing.

Listen to the Fire,
Crackling,
Hissing,
Popping.

Just Listen,
Take the Time,
Open Your Ears,
And Just Listen.

7

I sit down to write. When? Well, I try to do it everyday, but that doesn't always happen. That's how *Soothing Massage for the Mind* is. I'll write a couple pages, or maybe a quick thought here and there. *Soothing Massage for the Mind* is a collection of thoughts that I needed to paste together for all you lovely people to read. Much as life, you have things to paste together, or a puzzle to put together. This may take an entire lifetime, or you may be a lucky one and have that puzzle completed in your 20's. Maybe this book will help in the process. Some days, I have the flow and other days the river is dry. Then I remind myself that *Soothing Massage for the Mind* is a book to be a labour of love and love takes time sometimes.

Since I'm talking about when I write, I just want to touch on something that aggravates me a bit. I forget to write the dates on my poems and other writings. I was thinking of how I might have put this book in order, by dates. It would have shown how long it took me, but at the same time how crazy my mind works. Then I quickly changed my idea of that (and not 'cause I forgot dates) because of how I write. I'll write a little on something and I always feel I need to come back to it. Touch it up. Make it Perfect. So then I would have all these silly little Re-visited on this date and it just makes me laugh to even think about seeing that on a page. Plus, my writing is always a work in progress. A progress that I feel leaves me sometimes.

WHERE HAVE ALL THE POEMS GONE?

Where have all the poems gone?
Has love stolen Poetry's tongue?
Is there no more fantasy to bleed?
Are all the dreams of the depressed dead?
Did the secret sauce run dry?
Maybe the chain has been broken?
Or, sadness needs not to pour?
Maybe the tears are no more?
Or, time needs no record?
Does the pen just write nothing?
Is the mind finally clear?
Does no trouble mean no words?
Have they become a distant memory?
Did the glamour fade away?
Did all the muses die?
Did the pen not show up?
Or, did the paper get trashed?
Maybe the mind was napping?
Maybe the words are locked up?
Was it time to move on into Legend?
Are you just done with me?
Where have all the poems gone?

8

Sometimes I sit down to write and I find myself wanting to write about something I've written about before and I think to myself, "I don't want to be or sound redundant." Then that poses a problem of an almost chaotic paradox. You ask, "Why is that?" It's because the human race is redundant. It may sound sad, but it is all too true. Now no matter how hard you or someone you may know that tries not to be and loves change, will fall into that life of redundancy. It just seems to find us. Now this redundancy can be a million things from your favorite soda, favorite value meal, or always sitting in the back row of a movie theater. It's the little things we don't notice. Those pet peeves. I have a lot of those. That's a funny one. I'm not saying this is a bad thing. Sometimes it is a very good thing to have the things you feel need to be done everyday or every time you do a certain thing. It can make life comfortable. So, back to my writing, I don't mind writing something that is related to something else I have written because this time around I might put it in a different way. My word choice might be more appealing. It may have a different feel. There are many things that may happen so I just let it flow.

THE FLOW

What was I thinking?
Did I forget?
Maybe I wanted to,
Or am I losing it?

It's like a stream,
Constant,
Ever flowing,
Until the end.

But is there an end?
Opening to a delta,
To a whirlpool,
Where is the end?

It doesn't,
Just like my thoughts,
Flooding the land,
Ink upon my page.

So what was I thinking?
Did it matter?
Maybe another day?
Just going with the Flow.

9

Why must I feel so bad? Can I Stop? I think I wrote a poem about this a long time ago? To really think about it….Why have I been feeling like this for so long? Now….Can I make it Stop? Realize that it might not be. Be What? What is that Be? My Being? My Purpose? Am I to always Be this sad? Am I to always wallow in self pity? Can I say, "Fuck That"? "Fuck That, That's Not Me." I used to say, "Fuck It", but was that because I didn't care, or I cared so much it was beyond my help. How could something be beyond help that you care about? Many things, but it gets to the point of Enough is Enough. Now here is the thing…You come to the point…..

OKAY, I KNOW WHAT TO DO!

You come up with a game plan and you know if you can follow through with it…… YOU WILL COME OUT ON TOP. You will be happy and everything will be okay. Then this is what happens. You last a day or two and then something happens and you breakdown again. You know you don't want to be there. What is there to do? A Vicious Cycle that eats away at your whole being and essence.

So…… So….. So So So…How do we conquer this overbearing almost seemingly senseless rage? I feel you need help. I feel everyone needs help to a certain extent. How much help? Well, that would vary from person to person. It's good to have friends and your work and the little things you like to do. Then you'll have *Soothing Massage for the Mind*. Just think of me as a friend, a kind-hearted friend, a friend that will always be there for you.

This may seem like a bold statement of me being a great friend to you, but I'll put it into perspective for you. I'm sure you have had someone (a loved one, or parent) that told you that they would always be there for you and then that one day came and…they weren't. Now I'm not someone you have ever met or physically touched, but I will give you something far more important……WORDS. These words I write, these poems I share are something you can keep with you until the end of time. I just want *Soothing Massage for the Mind* (and the ones to follow this one) to be something that isn't picked up only once. I know I've picked up some books that as long as I live I will never pick up again. Hey, pick it up at least a few times. Thanks, I appreciate the couple of curls you just did. There are a few poems and songs that….I just hold dear to my heart. That helps me make it through the day, just for one line or maybe the entire thing. I just want to mention a few songs that might help you with your troubled mind. I do have a couple more books coming out, so they will have their own list. These songs are more or less to take you somewhere else and give your mind a break.

Queen - Was It All Worth It?
Sonata Arctica - Draw Me
Peter Gabriel - No Self-Control
Helloween - If I Could Fly
Michael Kiske - Do I Remember A Life?
Gnarls Barkley - Just A Thought
Arena -Don't Forget to Breathe or/ Friday's Dream
Eric Gales - Transformation

Some Instrumentals

Yanni - Twilight
Rick Wakeman - Sea Horses
Marty Friedman - Escapism
Keiko Matsui - Dream Walk
Erik Norlander - Sky Full of Stars

When it comes to Jazz and New Age artists, you can normally find that perfect CD that causes you to dim the lights and leave this world for a while. That's what people forget to do sometimes, they don't go out there and find great music, they think the radio is going to play it for them. That's not ever going to happen. Well, more in the next book. ☺ Always remember, when things get rough, just look for that Peaceful Endeavor.

MY PEACEFUL ENDEAVOR

Twisted is the Night,
Lying in Tears,
Choking down my Thoughts,
Mind on High.

Not tired enough,
I can't lie down,
Can't sleep,
It's too much.

Realizing,
What I Need,
More Mindless,
Waking Hours.

Maybe a favorite show,
A game of Solitaire,
Upon another game,
Just Something.

Blasting the music,
Trying to lose myself,
Leaving My Life,
Forgetting My Life.

My Tears Bleed,
All My Sadness,
All My Hate,
All My Pain.

Needing the Mindless Exhaustion,
To Ease My Heart,
And My Soul,
My Peaceful Endeavor.

10

I was planning on writing a bunch of "crying on your shoulder" type stuff here, but…I decided against it. ☺ So, I'm just going to paraphrase what I was planning on writing here. I was getting to the verge of 30 years old and before that I was going to have that infamous 10 year high school reunion. The fact of the matter, I didn't have anything to be proud of in my life. It's not the fact that I need to show off to someone, but that I didn't impress myself. Just the rundown: Failed marriage; Child support; No car; No money; No house (still at parent's house); I got fat; worked a horrible job and I'm sure I could add some more, but you get the point.

I was thinking about going to the reunion and bringing a little folder of poems I wrote just for the reunion. You know enough for everyone to have one. Maybe there was someone that was a publisher. Just dreaming, like a movie. I decided against it. Maybe by the time there is a 50th class reunion .... I might make it. LOL Well enough of that. How about a couple of those poems I would have brought with me.

REUNION

A Conversation Starts,
How have you been?
What have you done the past 10 years?

What have you become?

Questions You don't need,
Someone else to ask,
But Only the Important Ones,
You ask yourself Everyday.

Is this the Time to Share?
For Mockery,
For Rejoice,
Or just another day?

Maybe to see,
A Lost Friend,
An Old Enemy,
Or the Missing Love?

Do You Look at it as,
Another Step in Life?
Another Night Out?
A Rebirth?

Many Feelings will come,
Many will go,
Maybe Life will start again,
Or just Remain the same?

Maybe friends will be friends,
Maybe new eyes will meet,

Maybe it will be a waste of time,
That's for You to know.

So reach out Your Arms,
Raise a Glass,
Give a Cheer,
Because the Reunion is Here.

   Yeah, I know the last verse is a little cheesy, but….hey…..I
had to end the poem somehow.

And

HELLO

A Face crosses the Room,
With the same hair,
The same smile,
I know all too well.

It's been 10 years Now,
But for a second,
Yes a tiny second,
Time Stopped for Me.

It was a second of Eternity,
A Flame still Burning,
A Cup of Happiness,
A Cup of Sadness.

Then Time Returned to Me,
Back in my Seat,
Staring at My Lost Beauty,
Hoping for a Light.

Questioning Myself,
Will They see me?
Should I talk to them?
I came here for them?

Still sitting there,
Looking for the Courage,
As they walk up to me,
"Hello"

        Now, I know this one is more on the dreamy side. What can
I say....I live in Fantasyland.

11

The next poem I plan on sharing is a very deep poem. A poem I could easily put in one of my other two books, but I chose to put it in *Soothing Massage for the Mind* because it poses the question, WHY? When you deal with matters of the Heart and the essence of the Soul, you are always left with your Mind thinking about it. Your Mind is trying to figure it out or maybe your Mind is in the clouds. Nevertheless, your Mind can't stop thinking "WHY?" the rest of your body is feeling a certain way.

Back in High School, I liked a lot of girls, but there was one I was in love with. I wrote her quite a few poems and she loved my company, but she never wanted my love. I could never understand, WHY? Well, no sense in going into details, here's the poem.

WHY?

Sadness fills my heart,
And emptiness is my soul.
Tears are my eyes,
And bitterness is my tongue.

My heart had another heart,
And my soul attached to another soul.
My eyes were clear for another's eyes,
And my tongue was sweetness.

Our hearts seemed to be joyous,
And our souls seemed to match.
Our eyes were forever blue,
And our tongues meet only once.

Her heart didn't love.
Her soul ran away.
Her eyes looked no more,
And her tongue didn't say a word.

My heart is now lonely,
And my soul wondering, "Why?"
My eyes can't see straight,
And my tongue can not speak.

12

Some people write diaries. This isn't to say you have to be a writer to write a diary, no , not at all. Personally, I have never written in a diary. Unless, you count that one year in JR high or whenever it was in school. I heard that it was great for a writer to do that, and I have heard a lot of things. I do feel a diary can be useful to some people. It's a place you can let out all your cares and feelings and it's a friend that always listens.

Now writing can do certain things for you and may open new horizons. Most people don't write because they feel they can't or they have nothing important to say. That doesn't matter. Write about your day. You may enjoy it. You may find that it helps you. A Diary. A Record. It may help you from making the same mistake twice. May help to be a reminder of a Path you had (or was about to) gone down that was nothing but trouble. As far as I go, diaries aren't for me, but I write poems. I guess you could say that poems are my diaries. Just try writing about your day and see if it helps.

Well, since I'm talking about writing things down, I'm going to talk about something I should have written down. This lovely girl's name down. I was on this bus once, and I started talking to this great gal, and I got her number. Well, if I wasn't such a dumbass, I wouldn't have forgotten her name. So, why am I telling you this? Because…. That's what the next poem is about. I'm sure this is something that has happened to all of us. For your entertainment, my stupidity.

ABSENT MINDED

Am I so absent,
Of Mind,
Of Thought,
I forgot how to think?

Just a simple name,
A little reminder,
A Song,
A Verse.

Am I so far gone,
What's today?
Where's yesterday?
Lost in the future?

Am I that pathetic?
Just plain sorry?
Never clear,
Hoping for Sanity.

Can I forgive Me?
Will you forgive Me?
Next time I will try,
Not to be so Absent Minded?

13

I had a boss once (actually a new boss) at a job I had been doing for many years and she said to me, "Doug, I'm still trying to figure you out." I think I said something like, "Good luck, that's never going to happen."

It made me laugh because I could have said a million things in response, but hey I didn't want to be rude. That's not my style. Plus, I didn't know if she would have gotten my sense of humor. I feel that I'm pretty simple, but to others, I'm probably very complicated to them. They just don't understand the simplicity in my complexity. Even to this day…as old as I am…I still can't figure out myself sometimes. I just try to have a few guidelines to keep me sane. Those guidelines are what I leave up to others to figure out. I could tell you what kind of person I am, but that might make you fall in love with me. ☺

Of course, if a shrink read some of my poems, they would probably have a field day. And, all those blotted papers are demons or something dealing with sex, right? J/K That was a joke. Man, lighten up will ya!?! I meant demons doing sexual things. Okay, enough of that, how about another poem.

RIGHT, WRONG……WRONG, RIGHT

It must be Christmas,
For I have found a blank page,

To write a tale of wrong and right,
A vision for both,
The Good,
The Evil,
Both sides can see it,
What's wrong,
What's right,
Or Maybe what's wrong with the right,
Or what's right with the wrong?
It's always a matter of an opinion.
An Idea,
A Thought.
Who is to say what opinion is?
Is it wrong?
Is it right?
Why should we believe a many-handed God?
Why should we believe a supernatural God?
Why should we believe in anything?
Is it to have an opinion,
Cause you can't form one of your own?
Is it because you were told to,
And what was right and wrong,
Was forced upon you?
What's Right?
What's Wrong?
These things belong to you,
Your Heart,
Your Mind,
Your Soul,

A feeling through Your Whole Body,
This will tell you what to do,
It's not a matter of good and evil,
Right,
Wrong,
Let Yourself Free.

I kinda wrote this poem, in the angst of everyone putting their values on everyone. I really don't care what your religion is, or what you believe, just don't push it. Plus, don't act all rude when you don't want to hear someone else's idea. I really have a whole other book about this, but that's what is special about the human race. We have ideas and thoughts, and we should be able to share them, but not force them. Moving on with Them, or They?

WHAT THEY SAY

Life can get better,
Right?
At least,
That's what they say.

Of course,
They say many things,
"Life's what you make it,"
"Don't let Life get you down."

I could write them all,
And laugh at them all,
But is that it,
Life's a joke?

Have I laughed too long,
And missed important,
Moments?
Decisions?

Then there's no time machine,
No turning back,
Just to keep laughing,
Lying in misery.

Then I go back to,
What they say,
"Look on the Brighter side."
"You still have time."

Then I stop,
My Laughing,
Start Worrying,
Start Crying.

Then Laugh it off,
Once Again,
Blown Off,
Time Wasted.

I know,
I can't wait,
No more laughing,
No more crying.

I don't need,
Them to tell me,
What to do,
But instead,
I'll tell them,
And they'll say,
"That's What He Said."

That's what they say and then you get mad because you don't
want to hear any shit they have to say. So the whole time they are
talking you are trying to keep your cool. Hmm, turn the page to see if
you can feel the coolness.

KEEP MY COOL

Keeping my cool,
With fits in my head,
Driving me mad,
But why show it?

It wouldn't help,
I can't breakdown,
I can't afford the lost,
Just keep my cool.

Can I run away?
To go where?
Still having fits,
Driving me mad.

My help is clueless,
Or I'm clueless to help.
Either way doesn't matter,
Just keep my cool.

Is pretending the best?
Lie, lie, lie,
It's not me,
But I don't want the agony.

Lift my mask,
It keeps me cool,
Keeps the evil out or in,
I don't remember anymore.

Trying to keep my cool,
Weaker everyday,
Missing my sunshine,
Dying in darkness.

14

Here I am, again, another late night up and my Mind running like the Energizer Bunny. This becomes a problem when you aren't a professional writer and you have to get up at 5 in the morning for that job you love oh so much. I hardly ever go to bed with nothing on my Mind. I guess I could become a drunk and when I go to bed all I would have to worry about would be if the room was gonna stop spinnin'. Of course, booze isn't really high on my list to drink. So, how do I deal with my crazy Mind? I normally do a few things and two of them don't really help much when I have to go to work in the morning.

1) Stay up watching T.V. until I pass out.

2) Stay up playing on the computer until my eyes burn out.

And the last one which is a little bit more helpful.

3) Try to lay down an hour early and let my Mind run it's crazy course and I pass out.

I know some people take sleeping pills and may have other methods, but what works for you? I could probably offer suggestions all day long, but it really comes down to the individual. Everything in this book is to ease your Mind. Whether it's my mindless babble, or a line of poetry that gets you through the day. Here's some more pieces of my crazy Mind.

DOUGLAS DODD

WHAT I DID?

What I did?
What I didn't do?
What I should of done?
What I shouldn't have done?

It's a fine line,
Between Joy or Despair,
A flip of a coin,
For Rags or Riches.

Where's the time machine?
Will I do it right?
Is next time the same?
Just a vicious cycle?

Is probability against me?
Has Lady Luck died?
Did I kill the Albatross?
Where's my Ace of Spades?

Which way is Up?
How far Down must I go?
Is there any help?
Will my Choices be Clear?

To continue on the crazy train of poems, I have two that deal with the voices in my head. I feel like everyone probably talks to themself and I know I've had a million conversations with myself. Sometimes of future interactions I would like to have or maybe of something that I held my tongue on before because I was being nice. So in these two poems, can you figure out who is whom in each line?

WRITER'S BLOCK

A Blank sheet of paper,
Staring back at me.
Daring my mind,
Tempting my soul.
"Write Something!"
Taunting me with it's evil gaze.
"Say Something with meaning!"
"Do You need help?"
"HAHA, There's no help for you!"
There it goes again,
Line after Line,
Haunting my every thought.
What shall I write?
Love, Hate, Sorrow, Hope.

"Yes Decisions you should make."
But once again the Problem lingers,
So Many things to write,
And shall I write them all at once,
Or just stare at blank lines?
I could write of lines past,
Or maybe of lines of the future.
Maybe lines of the moment
Of what I'm thinking now?
Nothing at all and everything at once.
If only I could concentrate.
"Emptiness is your Head."
Again the lines abuse me,
And again I'm more determined.
"Then WRITE and shock us."
Yes I will because I can.
For what may seem like Nothing,
Can mean Something. "In Deed."

AND

"DO SOMETHING"

All the eyes are upon You,
"Do Something!"

There goes the mockery,
"You know it!"
I look around for something,
Someone to help me,
"They're Gone."
What?
"It's only Me."
That voice again,
Only there to hurt me.
"No, I'm Not!"
Why?
What do you want?
"To push You."
Into a Deep Dark Hole?
"No."
What, then?
"Forward, stupid!"
Then let me be.
"It's not that easy."
I know.
"You Do?"
Yes,
I Do,
Or should I say, "You Do, too."
What do You mean?
"You're Me. I'm You."
Then that would be easy.
"How would that be?"
I could turn off.

"Not if I'm You, and You Me."
Oh No!
"Well, turn Me off!"
I Can't!
"Do Something!"

15

I think (truly) just a poem or a song is just good enough to help someone make it through the day. At least, that's what I've heard from some people. I had a friend once that told me that all he needed to was read one line from one of my poems and he was set for the rest of the day. At first, I found that funny….well…no…more insulting because I want my whole poem read and then, " Hey, tell me about it? What did you think?" Then he would say that that one line is sometimes so powerful and so meaningful that it is all he needs to help him make it through the day. Then I would be cool with it. I know everyone is different and everyone deals with heartache, love, family, business, and whatever else that may come their way differently. Just as I write this book, that's how I cope with my life, and it may help you, too. So now let's do some Reflecting

REFLECTING

Reflecting upon another day,
And it's just like the last,
But I've learned how to breathe,
And no longer gasp on tears.

Maybe it's better that way,
Just having myself,

And all the knowledge,
That I'm a true pain in the ass.

Being set in my ways,
And pondering the compromise,
But I'm at the point of living,
And don't need the nit pick.

Don't need to Love,
The things that bother me.
Don't need worrying about fixing,
The things that bother you.

Maybe I'll Reflect on a future day,
To see how my ways are being set,
Then my need won't be compromised,
And Nothing will need to be fixed.

16

Some days can be really hard when you let your mind take you on a ride and the rollercoaster never seems to stop. That's why I write. I hope that when I write, that rollercoaster will stop, well, at least for the moment. It might help me for an hour, or day, or maybe a week. Then I can get my focus back on track. It's all about staying on your path and not chasing that rabbit down it's dark hole. The next two poems are dealing with my mind running away with my thoughts.

BREAKDOWN COMING

Tossing and turning,
Holding it all in,
Trying to keep it together,
But that breakdown's coming.

It's coming to finally,
Shatter   me   to   nothing.
And there's nothing I can do,
Because my needs aren't met.

Needs that have always,
Been floating over my head,

But continue to drift,
As I help everyone else.

I've had many breakdowns,
And I've always kept walking,
But I'm in fear of this one,
If I can't control it?

I'm falling apart,
Piece by Piece,
Too tired to fight,
That Breakdown Coming.

AND

THE MELTDOWN OF MY MALFUNCTION

So it's another day of insanity,
But the meltdown of my malfunction,
Is just how I bleed,
Some more words for you.

At this point,
Who thinks who's more crazy,

You of I,
Or Me of Me?

It's easy to run away,
But really is that real,
And where's the fun,
And will something be missed?

I know I could write,
A million words of longing,
And for some it's lost,
And others totally get it.

But writing my perfect love,
Is far different than receiving,
And yet I'm ready to give,
And yet you hold back.

So begins my day of insanity,
Within the meltdown of my malfunction,
Taking more trips through my life,
And I shake my head in coincidence.

17

Have you ever thought about traveling to another plane of existence or dimension? Maybe the answers for life are there. Maybe on another world in outer space. Maybe it's just me letting my mind wander.

GOING THROUGH ANOTHER DAY

Going through another day.
"Why am I here?"
"What is the point?"
Wondering if it really is,
A question of being,
When the world,
Doesn't seem to care.
When it's all about,
Money!
Power!
Looks!
When the government,
Doesn't care if you live.
Land of the Free,
Free from What?

That phrase has no meaning.
So back to the existentialism,
Of this poem,
And how that word,
Has a different meaning.
It can't be answered,
With any pure existence,
Well...unless I,
Leave my life,
And take that spiritual journey,
But that's not what I'm talking about,
It's about Me,
And not someone else.
Maybe I ask,
The questions,
That can't be answered.
Maybe I ask,
The questions,
That need another life?
Maybe the answers,
Are on another dimension?
Maybe the answers,
Are Just Going Through Another Day.

18

The next couple of poems deal with you asking yourself, "What is it that I want?" There comes a time in your life that you have to stop what you are doing and think, what do I want? What is it that gets me excited about someone else? What is me? What are you to me? Now, I could probably go on and on with this and I have in many poems, but for now I just have two to share.

WHAT IS IT THAT I LOVE?

What is it that I love?
And what is true,
And what is false,
And what can I really believe?

Is it the idea of butterflies,
That may really mean plain arousal?
Is it the thought of sweet kisses,
That I could give to anyone?

Maybe it's me waking to a smile,
And not that of a beautiful face,
But a smile upon my face,

That is pure for the whole world to see?

Never feeling a fit of depression,
Because I was able to clear my mind,
But that means coming to terms,
With all that troubles me.

Can I make a commitment to myself?
Can I follow through with plans?
Hell, can I really make plans?
If not, my life is just a waste.

So, Love is just a fable,
And I'm too much a fool,
Daydreaming and wishing life away,
Only to realize my own misguidance.

What is it that I love?
Might has past me,
And yet has truly met me,
But we know of our souls?

Maybe there are different soulmates,
For each life that we live,
And maybe there are many,
That all connect to one.

But what makes these bonds,
Will also break them.

So where is the unbreakable bond,
Or is that something that's eternal?

Life After Life,
Always coming across Souls,
Usually the same ones,
But Life and Time fails you?

Eternally Locked.
Mortally Flawed.
Forever Fated.
Always Troubled.

What is it that I love?
The true facade of my delusions,
Always laughing at me,
Fueling all the dark sarcasm deep within.

Is it all the fantasies,
All the could-have-beens,
Or it's really more so the wishlist,
Endless nights begging on empty dreams.

But when will I go out of my way,
And finally realize it's no problem,
That it's something that goes with the flow,
As my hand through my love's hair.

Will I feel my heart beat with yours?
Will it be in unison,

Or will they beat as if it was a race,
And will you hold my hand for the ride?

What is it that I love?
The thought of how much I can,
But forever in search of,
Dying to give it all away.

It's to write that one last line,
The Words of the Poem to End all Poems,
The Beauty, Heart, Soul, Sex, Smell, Eyes,
And All and Everything and Complete.

It's that cloudy dream,
And there's only one person you see,
With Eyes that see your True Soul,
And Lips calling you 'Love'.

What is it that I love?
It is so many things,
And yet nothing at all.
It's still locked inside my heart.

What is it that I love?
An Angel waiting to fly to me,
To cast away my demons,
And show me what it is that I love.

DOUGLAS DODD

AND

WHAT IS IT THAT MOVES ME?

What is it that moves me?
Your pretty smile?
Your sweet words?
Your soft touch?

It's everything about you,
And the thought,
Of what could be,
What I really want.

You're nothing but a pawn,
And I place you,
Here,
Or there.

I give you the words,
I speak your mind,
It's how you feel,
I give you the power.

Then you take it away,
Like a flash in the pan,

Never spoken,
Never held.

I wish upon your ear,
I dream of your gaze,
You give no mind,
Making me powerless.

It's all about me,
Wanting you,
Wanting me,
What should be?

My Dream,
Your Beauty,
My Mind,
You Moving Me.

19

This next poem I would like to talk about is gonna have to wait until after you read it. HAHA!!!

THE FORBIDDEN WORD

There I was,
I was about to do it,
Just one more push,
Just one more line to be crossed.

What was holding me back?
All I had to do was speak,
Those forgotten words,
The words lost in time and space.

Words I knew,
Words I couldn't use.
I didn't know the order.
I don't want to say I forgot.

More afraid of the magic,
It's glorious power,

It's devastating power,
The power of the unknown.

Will I feel great?
Will I be left destroyed?
Then I wonder,
Is it best unsaid?

It's a trick?
A mind over matter,
Like I always say,
"If you don't mind, it doesn't matter."

So why all the questions?
I know,
I'm a big pussy,
I can't help it.

Am I too nice?
Am I too shy?
I'll show you yours,
If you show me mine.

Is that right?
No, maybe?
Is that too much?
Is it deeper than we should be?
You tell me?

Maybe I think too much?
Maybe not enough?
If I thought more,
I would have all the answers?
You tell me?

I want to be able,
To speak freely.
Maybe never shutting up,
Maybe all too much.
And then complete silence.

Then what kind of silence will it be?
Comfortable?
Uneasy?
Dreadful?

Does this make sense?
To me,
Yes.
To you?

I can't wait for that understanding.
Do I try to analyze too much?
Am I wasting time?
Will I always waste time?
And all this for a simple...... HELLO.

This is probably something everyone can understand. It's one of those things, when you're in the coffee shop, or mall, or walking on the sidewalk and you see that beautiful face. A face that you want to know everything about, but gathering the courage to say something, or anything to that cute face on the other side of the room....first you have to say Hello. The million things that run through your mind as you think about saying that forbidden word. The word should start a conversation, but living in the world we do, that doesn't always happen. There are too many factors to warrant a conversation, but there shouldn't be. Most people feel that their time is far too important for useless babble. Sometimes you need that empty conversation. It may not be so empty, and you may feel good that you started talking. What's the worst thing that can happen, you have to go back to what you were doing? This poem flowed out on one of those many days and nights writing poems and stories at the coffee shop. Blackberry Italian Soda with Whip Cream. Maybe a vanilla frappe with whip cream and cinnamon on top. Just doing some people watching and thinking...How do You say "Hello?"

20

I've finally reached the point where I have gotten tired of speaking and feel that I should just share poems. I still have a little bit more to say, but for the most part you will finally get to read poem after poem. The main reason for *SOOTHING MASSAGE FOR THE MIND*. They are only one part of my life's journey, as you will see in my next books to come. I have broken the rest of my poems down into 7 Categories. I've given each category a name from a favorite song of mine and a little synopsis, so you will know what you are in store for.

DREAMER
(Europe - Wings of Tomorrow)

In this section, I have poems about dreams or ideas that someone may have about their life. It's like when someone tells me to be positive or just says something positive to me, I'm like, "Well, that's wishful thinking." The thing is...always try to hold on to something that motivates you.

DREAM

Let your mind free,
Dream of your dreams.
Don't try so hard,
Leave your worries behind.
Just for a few moments,
Let space and time set you free.
Dream of fields of butterflies,
And flowers colored by the rainbow.
Dream of an ocean blue,
Where the dolphins dance and sing.
Dream of an icy mountain top,
Where the eagles fly free.
Dream of the deepest of space,
Where another world greets you.
Dream of your home,
Where love is everlasting.

Dream a little Dream,
Just to give you peace of mind.

A DREAM TO ESCAPE

How is it done?
Close Your Eyes,
Place Your Finger,
Upon a Map?

Your Final Destination?
A New Start,
A Happy Beginning,
To Refresh My Life?

Many Nights,
I Stare at the Map,
The World,
A Better Place.

Something To
Catch My Eye,
Ignite a Fire,
Touch My Soul.

Many Ideas,
What If
That's Possible,
A Dream to Escape.

Escape From
Those Dreadful Memories,
A Stagnant Life,
An Unwanted Grave.

The Journey has
Been Laid Down
Many Times,
Only to Fail.

Now Can I Be,
Brave,
Take that Step,
Truly Be Free?

My Burdens
Will Always Be,
But I Need to Live,
A Dream to Escape.

FOREVER

The hot summer evening,
Seems to turn into an icy nightmare,
As I wrap myself into my blanket,
And clutch my pillow.

"The loneliness is too much,"
I sometimes think.
I wish I had someone to hold,
Someone to share my feelings.

I long for that love,
Love of forever giving.
I always greet it with open arms,
But it always runs on by.

One day I do pray,
That it will stop,
And hold me forever,
Forever, forever, and forever.

I LOOK OUT THE WINDOW

I look out the window,
Dreams in my head,
Everywhere I turn,
Along with sadness.

Allowing things,
To get me down,
Trouble my mind,
And weaken my heart.

Then there's my soul,
Still with some will,
Still with some attitude,
But the drive is slow.

The waiting is smothering,
Hard to breathe,
Hard to dream,
Dying a little everyday.

Needing some spark,
My rejuvenation,
Until then,
I'll look out the window.

IMAGES

The repetition of images,
The voices and sounds,
They awake my mind to no end,
Don't know if they're real or fantasy.

The images stay with me day and night,
I walk into rooms,
And no one says a word,
But I still hear voices of distant ones.

Even the empty rooms bring the images,
And I lay there thinking,
Thinking if they will ever end,
Or are they supposed to be my companions?

My mind is always in thought,
The conversations never end,
The birds never stop chirping,
And the wind never stops swirling.

I pray to God,
For one day to show my mind calm,
If not calm, the way in which,
All my images can be one with my mind.

STAY

Skin so soft,
Hair so long,
Eyes so kind,
Will this Stay so?

A touch too warm,
A word too nice,
A look too shy,
Will this Stay too?

Hearts that are full,
Minds that are thinking,
Feelings that are longing,
Actions that are to Stay?

Can Love Stay?
Can Eternity Stay?
Can Souls Stay?
Can all this Stay?

DOUGLAS DODD

STANDSTILL

Again at a standstill,
Not knowing,
What to do,
Where to go.

Still there,
Wanting it all,
Wanting it now,
But left empty.

Having to start over,
Again and again,
Or maybe never did,
Just my illusion.

Constantly thinking,
Of another way,
Another downfall,
Needing something.

A standstill forever,
Forever wanting,
Now Never,
Soon Enough.

WRITING ON THE WALL
(Blackmore's Night - Shadow of the Moon)

Sometimes there are signs that just hit you from out of the blue and sometimes you are completely blinded to everything. Sometimes you write yourself little messages to remind you. Sometimes you write something down to only forget it. So, what was written on your wall?

LOVE₁

Is true Love out there?
A question that comes,
Too often to the mind.
It tortures me so.

Am I too picky to see it?
Another question to ponder,
It suits me too well.
It's the way I see.

Is there a woman good enough?
A woman that Loves me,
As great as I Love?
Another question in the sky.

Love?

IT

Is It indecision?
Is It jealousy?
Is It right?
Is It wrong?

Can It be filled?
Can It be resolved?
Can It be found?
Can It be fixed?

Will It be true?
Will It be love?
Will It be forever?
Will It be so?

How is It real?
How can It be?
How will It stay?
How is It..... IT?

WORDS ESCAPE ME

Words escape me,
No reason why,
Just another face,
How are you special?

What makes me special?
Is that important?
Our Specialties?
Just simple smiles?

Are glances good enough?
A hand shake?
Hello?
How are you?

Are you shallow?
Or Deep?
Would you like help?
Or can you give?

Should I think?
Or be mindless?
What do you think?
Is it me?

Just to crack a smile,
Seems hard,
But will you,
And only you?

SLEEP

Not wanting to sleep,
Another Black Hole,
The useless distraction,
What can I do?

Coffee doesn't help,
Walk another mile?
Does anything Work?
Just Sleep.

Go to another world,
Feel Free Again,
You're in Control,
All You have to do is Sleep.

NO! I always come back,
Back to Nothing,
Back to the Living,
Only a Pain of Dying.

But Sleep loves all,
Dream to be fulfilled,
Dreams deep within,
Just close your Eyes.

Dream of a New Day,
Dream of New Love,
Sleep for Me,
Waking for You.

THEM

Will they run?
Will they cry?
Are words enough?
Or just too much?

Do they know?
Do they care?
Are actions enough?
Or just too much?

Can they see?
Can they hear?
How much is enough?
How much is too much?

What will make them stop?
Whist will make them love?
What is just enough?
What is too perfect?

WHAT IS SO HARD

What is so hard
About letting go?
What is so hard
About moving on?

Is it the security?
The daily routine?
A peace of mind,
Knowing everyday is the same?

Then one day changes,
Life set off course,
As the storm rages,
Can you keep from washing away?

Should you hold on,
With a death grip?
Should you let go,
And travel to the unknown?

LEFT WITH ONLY DUST

Always looking for some purpose,
Some reason,
Never happy,
Is there more?

Am I truly never satisfied?
Can I be happy?
Can I set myself free?
Why do I feel the leash?

Can I cut the rope?
Break the chain?
Or am I too weak?
Maybe just give up?

Are there really signs,
That are plain to see?
Maybe I forgot,
Or always turn my head?

Am tired of asking "Why?"
It never helps,
But what am I to do,
Lie there broken?

Where do my pieces go?
I fell too fast,
And too hard,
Left with only dust.

WHAT'S ON YOUR MIND (PURE ENERGY)
(Information Society - Information Society)

It's those moments when you are all alone and have nothing, but your thoughts. The power of the brain can be very overwhelming. For me, I have a million thoughts sometimes on just one idea and then my pen is off to the races. What do you do with your mind energy?

MY QUESTIONS

Do I have the strength,
To walk through the day?
Will my voice stay clear,
To say what's on my mind?

Can I open my eyes,
To see another face?
Can my eyes,
Truly see again?

Do I know,
The right words to say?
Who will save me,
From my unknown thoughts?

Does it matter,

What I wear?
Does it matter,
If my hair is cut?

Can I look into your eyes,
And not feel ashamed?
Can I touch you,
And not run in fear?

What I like,
Is that for you?
Will one day come,
Where I don't have to worry about my questions?

WHY AM I ME?

Why am I me?
Is it for torture?
Was I evil in my past life,
And this is my sentence?

Does Love Matter?
Is it just misery?
Can't stop looking,
At the forever dead-end.

Should I give in,
Say it's true,
"I'll never be happy,"
Save my pity.

No one understands,
I can't function,
Everything hurts,
Why am I me?

AWKWARD

What would please You?
I'm easy,
Let me help,
I don't want much.

What do you want?
I'll buy it,
Steal it,
I'll find it somehow.

Are you easy going?
Here or there,
Up or down,
Just wanting to smile.

Needing to take some time?
Healing an open wound,
Protecting a secret love,
A Mask to reveal.

We can still be happy,
Give me a wink,
I'll share my hand.
It's a funny world.

GOOD ENOUGH

Am I good enough?
Is the standard too high?
Is it my standard?
Is it theirs?

I still wonder,
What is enough?
Still unfulfilled,

Still wanting more.

Can I reach,
That mountain,
That plateau,
That pinnacle of Mine?

Is anyone good enough?
Or are they all,
Good enough for me,
And my set ways?

Do I need to change?
Should I have to?
There's nothing wrong,
I'm Good Enough, right?

IT'S DREAM

Did I forget?
Did I remember?
Or was It time,
And I wasted too much?

Always Waiting,
Always putting off
That next step,
And what It takes?

Do I have It in me?
Or Course,
Yeah,
Why Not?

The bumbling questions,
A nagging paranoia,
That's all a dirty hat,
Needing to be tossed.

Holding on to It,
But not living It,
Or running with It,
Just longing It's Dream.

WHAT DOES IT ALL MEAN?

The emptiness,
The truth,
The inner self,
What does it all mean?

The lie,
The right,
The wrong,
What does it all mean?

The game,
The trial,
The match,
What does it all mean?

To step forward,
To step back,
To stay,
What does it all mean?

I Don't Know!

DOUGLAS DODD

JUST LET ME KNOW

Yes
No
Maybe
Well if I wasn't in this position.

How should I feel?
Answers never clear.
Heart and Mind,
Always at War.

Forgot what was right,
Lost all feeling,
Should I try?
Should That be an option?

Maybe it was never meant to be easy,
Looking for a solution,
Any kind of formula,
Never one to appease.

Yes
No
Maybe
Well.....just let me know.

TOO MUCH TIME ON MY HANDS
(Styx - Paradise Theatre)

I sometimes wonder how some writers, actors, or musicians can produce so much in like a year. Then I think, well, they must really use their time wisely. Of course, they don't have to go to some shitty 40 hour job that takes up all their time. Then, I still feel like I waste too much of my time doing mindless things. Either way, I don't think you could have too much time on your hands.

DOES IT HELP?

Does it help?
Really?
Another Line?
Another Poem?

I'm still left with me,
Miserable,
Lonely,
Depressed.

Looking for something,
Love,
Peace,
Happiness.

Am I the fool,
With shaky hands,
Blistered feet,
A hardened heart?

Do I need all the weight?
Does it make me stronger?
Only weaken,
Day by Day?

How much must one give?
Is All,
Not good enough?
Where is that line?

I write to ease my mind,
But does it help?
I write to ease your mind,
Does It Help?

NOT MUCH INSPIRED

Not Much Inspired.
Can't feel the Flow.
Where did it Go?
Is it Gone?

Why can't I have…
A good day?
A nice time?
A peaceful thought?

What will set me free?
Is it too deep?
It is so shallow?
Is it all in my mind?

Lost in thought.
Eyes wondering.
Legs shaking.
Finger tapping.

Looking for that spark.
Maybe not today,
Maybe later,
Not Much Inspired.

DOUGLAS DODD

WHEN?

When was the last time?
The last time of anything,
Love felt throughout,
A peace of mind?

When will the next time be?
The next soulful touch,
Enlightenment of the spirit,
A sweet kiss?

Is all the effort mine?
Effortlessly into nothing,
Smiles changing to frowns,
A happy thought?

Where does the road end?
This road to eternal bliss,
Where my feet don't hurt,
A new land?

When will I rest my bones?
Bones needing a soft caress,
Pure and True,
My beautiful bed?

WAITING

Is it Right?
This Waiting Game?
My Life passing by,
Not able to live.

Another Chain,
Holding Me Back,
Another Wall,
Blocking My Way.

Invisible it all may be,
But Strong and Firm.
My fight becoming,
A faint whimper.

Waiting for Strength,
Waiting for Faith,
Waiting for .....
That Open Door.

Patience becoming a burden,
Procrastination never a friend,
Lost in Time,
Waiting for the right ride.

DOUGLAS DODD

OUT OF SIGHT, OUT OF MIND

Out of Sight,
Out of Mind,
Do I belong here?
Where should I go?

Thoughts of the abnormal.
Feelings of being misplaced.
Why am I so different?
Is this my time?

Looking for my dream.
Clinging on to my separation.
Where is my home?
Does someone own it?

Wanting an escape,
But trapped in my world.
Can I erase my heavy thoughts?
Does everything have a bleak outlook?

Closing My Eyes,
One More Time,
Out of Sight,
Out of Mind.

STOP MY WASTING AWAY

I don't need strength to walk the days,
It's easy to coast along,
I really need is some confidence,
Otherwise, I just amount to nothing.

Steps are hard to take,
Fighting a mind that tells me,"No",
All the while my soul says, "Yes",
But my heart surrenders the chance.

I'm not living my life true,
To my prospective or philosophy,
It's not even set guidelines,
But maybe I should really have some?

A million people could all cheer,
"We know you can do it",
And it's still only background noise,
Because fear doesn't allow my cheer.

Every day and night,
I look around every corner,
Maybe there's an easier way,
But I know there's no other way.

I must take the hard road,
I must look forward to live,
Don't let fear breed hate,
Stop my wasting away.

ONLY TIME WILL TELL

Did I really say "Goodbye" ?
Did I really have my final say?
Can I remember that last moment?
Do I need closure?

Things I wonder about,
Things that have come and gone,
Were we really friends?
Who didn't care first?

Who was the one to stop calling?
Who didn't stop by anymore?
Do you really want to see me?
Do I really want to see you?

Is it a burden I need?
Will a weight be lifted?
There is one thing for sure,
Only Time Will Tell.

INFORMATION OVERLOAD
(Living Colour - Time's Up)

Have you ever had one of those days that everything gives you a sensory overload? Yeah, I know… "I don't want to Adult today." But, sometimes you need to find a way around the pile of garbage being set in front of you. Maybe a paper shredder will help?

MATHEMATICS

Mathematics?
You got to be a raving psychotic,
It's easy for awhile,
Just dealing with numbers,
Then you get into,
Those letters and variables,
Going crazy 'cause,
You don't see numbers.

So the teach rearranges,
Your brain,
And those letters and variables,
Seem like numbers now,
And you think to yourself,
"I've become a Raving Psychotic."

IDEA

A light bulb,
An Idea,
Where do they come from?
Where do they go?

They appear,
As quickly as they vanish,
As the breeze,
Touches your face.

Always reaching,
Wanting a full grasp,
To hold forever,
And never let go.

Transparent,
But Whole,
Endless,
But Forgotten.

A grassy plain,
Or a thunderous night,
Maybe a raging sea,
Can you see it?

It could be a nap,
Or a stroll in the park,
Or even that Sunday drive,
Where is your Idea?

I THOUGHT

I thought I came to write,
I thought I came to chill,
I thought I could get away,
I thought this time would be different,
I thought I would find someone,
I thought I wouldn't dream,
I thought "why do I do this",
I thought of nothing good,
I thought about getting lost in the music,
I thought that's the only way,
I thought I could leave forever,
I   thought   it   would   be   easy,
I thought why bother with love,
I thought "it only kills",
I thought of a beautiful day,
I thought of another world,
I thought of a time gone by,
I thought of what's in me,
I thought of the sorrow,

I thought of the pain,
I thought of the happiness I want,
I thought and I thought.

HAVE I BEEN HAD

Have I been had,
Again?
Is my heart that big,
Or Soft?

Just left in Confusion,
Wondering,
What's going on?
Did I have a choice?

Never in good position,
Always out of line,
Missing a break,
Maybe it's too late.

Maybe I have it all wrong,
I finally can
Make that Difference,
Be the One on Top.

No More Black Days,
Let the Sun break free,
Wash my face,
And Smile Again.

WHAT IS LIFE?

What is Life?
Errors and Mistakes?
Or the Right Place and Time?

What is Life?
Pain and Suffering?
Or the Healing and Giving?

What is Life?
War and Abuse?
Or is it Peace and Harmony?

What is Life?
Hate and Loneliness?
Or is it Love and Happiness?

What is Life?
But everything in between,
And everything throughout.

ALL IN MY MIND

Is it all in my mind?
Those mental blocks?
My twitching nerves?
Questions for Questions?

Just poke me,
See if I'm alive,
Still breathing,
Hear me speak.

Does anyone care?
Maybe they're just annoyed,
At my constant thought,
Wondering in Oblivion.

Believing in Nothing,
Hoping for Everything,
Faith and Love,
Dancing in the Dark.

Another imaginary friend,
Who needs you?
I'll think for my friend,
Never a dull conversation.

Adventures are endless,
Stories to tell,
Everyone needs me,
My Mind Open.

Raped of feelings,
Lost in space,
Too many paths,
Never clear.

I'll take you,
On another trip,
Just hold on,
It's All in My Mind.

THE PUZZLE

My life is just a puzzle,
Looking where the pieces fit.
Will I get it done in time,
But is there a time frame?

Should I come up with a gameplan,
Or just see if the pieces fall?
Should I work on my edges,
Or from the center outward?

What if I stare at a piece too long,
Or neglect a section too long?
What if I ram the wrong piece in,
And then the perfect piece has no home?

I could always throw the puzzle away,
But where would that leave me?
Looking for another puzzle to finish,
When I still have one undone?

I must use some patience for myself.
Let the pieces find their proper places.
Until all the pieces make the puzzle whole.
Each empty space is my unfinished journey.

MADNESS CAUGHT ANOTHER VICTIM

(Evergrey - Recreation Day)

Madness!?! Come one and come all. LMAO Can you feel the evil? No, not really, it doesn't always have to be evil to be Madness. Maybe? Right? I don't know, but will you be the judge, or be the one caught.

SUSAN SHAW

I didn't know Susan Shaw,
But no one really knew her,
In sense of the friendly side,
Which was not her side,
Why she didn't like people,
Could be she hated herself,
Maybe that's why she's six feet under,
She didn't kill herself nicely,
She could have cut her wrists,
It would have been prettier,
But she put a spike in her head,
To put a point on things.

THE ROOM

I walk into a room,
Full of a million voices.
Starting off as whispers,
Then louder and louder.

As I turn to leave,
The door is gone,
And the walls close in,
Making the noise pierce me.

As I blink my eyes,
I'm in a room of light.
That hurts my eyes,
With any slight movement.

I try to shade them,
To look for an off switch.
Only to see bare walls,
And a personal hell.

Sometimes the voices,
Don't Stop.
Sometimes the lights,
Won't Turn Off.
Sometimes my eyes,
Deceive Me.
Sometimes my thoughts,

Make Me Crazy.
Sometimes I need,
Some Peace.

IS THERE?

Is there love left?
To a heart so weighted,
To a heart in pieces,
To a life of ruin.

Is there any fight left?
To a spirit so battered,
To a spirit in waste,
To a thought of surrender.

Is there any happiness left?
To a soul so weathered,
To a soul in pain,
To a life of sadness.

Is there any hope left?
To a mind so spent,
To a mind in grief,
To a thought of despair.

Is there anything left?
Is there any will left?
Is there anybody left?
Only time will tell.

QUESTIONS

How much heart can one have?
A question that,
That may never be answered,
But pondered forever.

How many tears can one release?
Another question to be pondered.
Will the rain ever stop,
Falling for an eternity?

Is love to be obtained?
Just an optimistic question,
When love isn't yours,
A fading dream?

Is it any good to care?
A question to ask,
When the care is never given.

The "Who Cares" attitude.

What is life for?
The big question,
When one has Love, Peace, and Happiness,
Something Made in Heaven?

TONIGHT

The moon hides,
In the clouds,
As if like a child,
Hiding under the covers.

A Crawling Darkness,
Chokes all light,
The grass,
Even gives a shiver.

Noises from behind,
Noises from there,
A Shadow moves,
A Howl is heard.

Is it my mind,
Maybe just my ears,

Maybe a Ghost?
Who is playing games?

Is it safe?
The walk home?
To go to my friend's?
To stay outside?

What's behind that tree?
Were those Red Eyes?
An Evil-Toothed Grin?
Or nothing at all?

Do I just get scared,
To only feed myself,
Of this boring life,
Of Nothingness?

Or is it that,
"What If" Factor?
People don't believe,
But shouldn't they?

It's only darkness,
But people don't know,
What I know,
Or What I see.

But now the moonshines,
A clear path is shown,

No Monsters are seen,
At least Not Tonight.

AM I SO SAD

Why must I go home?
Is there some place else?
Do I even have a friend?
Am I so sad?

Why must I work?
Can't I just get by?
Do I really need the headache?
Am I so poor?

Why must I love?
Is there only Hell?
Do I really need pain?
Am I so weak?

Why must I see?
Can't I just sleep?
Do I even have good sight?
Am I So Sad?

IT[2]

It slowly eats at you,
Day by Day.
Like a festering Sore,
Little by Little.

It comes in many Forms,
From Sadness to Loss of Time,
From Anger to Utter Tears,
It eats away your whole being.

It's a silent killer.
You're one of It's many victims,
Like a puppet on a string,
And It's your Master.

It's a deep dark Funk,
A Swamp of Sorrows.
It's the quicksand,
That slowly sucks you down.

It's the Monster you feared.
It's the only thing you can't stop.
It's all You have,
Can you become It's Master?

DOUGLAS DODD

THE DARK RIDE
(Helloween - The Dark Ride)

The thoughts within your head can take you on a wild ride. It doesn't always show you a pleasant ride, but sometimes it may show you a little glimpse of happiness...or you just plain go crazy. These next poems are going on that dark ride to....who knows, and who knows when that train is going to stop. So you can put that seat belt on, or just hold onto the handle and pray you don't fly off. Full speed ahead!

TRY

A walk through the park,
More like a mine-field,
With every step being deadly,
When I think of having your love.

Why do you make it so hard?
Why do you reject me so?
Why don't you want love?
Why won't you let yourself go?

Are you running away?
Away from love?
Away from it coming to an end?

Away from what you don't understand?

Do you feel for something else?
There's something better?
There's something cuter?
There's something less complex?

Why won't you try?
The comfort of warmth.
The sweet taste of love.
The soul at rest.

The mind at release.
The feeling of security.
The heart full of joy.
Why won't you try?

LIES

How far back can a Lie go?
The Beginning?
The Middle?
The End?

Were all the truths Lies?

How will I know?
Will I ever know?
Should I even care?

Is the pain just enough?
Or do I need the sharp dagger?
Tiny Little daggers,
Tiny Little Lies.

When have I bled enough?
Once my body's an empty shell,
Filled up again,
Bleed again.

Was too late soon enough?
Or sooner really later,
Time wasted,
Time to regain.....from Lies.

THE CATCH

It's the Catch,
Number 22,
The rift in space,
Shifting time.

So easily is our minds,
Toyed with,
Even tortured,
Dreams lived to be burned.

Out of the ashes,
Or another trail of smoke,
A distant signal,
Or your own disallowance.

Build on memories,
Shattered in a moment,
The bright side,
Or a dark secret.

The eagerness to reach,
The stubbornness to stop,
Opening that door,
Or maybe keeping it closed.

Caught by the Catch,
Seeing the sign,
The number's in your eyes,
One Open...One Closed.

DOUGLAS DODD

WHAT'S THE POINT

What's the point,
In this waste of time?
A damn idleness,
Dusk over dawn.

Tides in and out,
Another sunrise,
A changing moon,
Waiting equals Wasting.

Is it to just relax,
From that hateful job,
A nagging family,
Time not stopping.

Putting things off,
For something more perfect,
An easier life,
To only waste more time.

So what's the point,
In finding time to kill?
Free moments gone,
And never regained.

I FORGOT

The scars too deep,
Can't wear the mask,
No more smiles,
Somehow forgot.

All the walls are up,
In an empty room,
Myself Raped,
And Alone.

There's no way out,
Maybe In,
I don't know,
I forgot.

My attempts to escape,
Only fail,
Adding to my demise,
My Solitude.

Now my hands,
To my face,

A Final Blink,
A Final Sigh.

ONCE AGAIN

Once again I'm looking for a dark place,
But do I only feel right there?
Am I really digging out of a hole,
Or am I just shifting the same dirt?

The many times I've looked at myself,
And every time I shake my head,
Because I'm still clueless as a two-year old,
With no idea what the signs say.

The years continue to roll on by,
As my life continues to die,
And the light in my eyes won't last,
But it's really all my fault, right?

I can't reach the controls,
Because the means were never learned,
But now I have no other choice,
And where do I put all this dirt?

Once again I will make another journey,
Maybe this time I will leave this dark place,
To stand on solid rock than loose dirt,
But will I truly feel right, then?

LOVE IS OUT THERE?

Another Corner,
To Turn.
Another Boulder,
To Rollover.

Is there an easy way?
Do I make it hard,
On Myself,
On Others?

Trying to be strong,
But my faith is thin.
Trying to hold on,
But the pieces fall quickly.

My Patience,
Had to be learned,
But quickly fade,
As each day passes.

Go Crazy,
Minute by Minute,
And What of the Otherside?
No Help.

Conversations,
Becoming Darker.
The End,
Becoming Clearer.

Just turn the corner,
Roll that boulder over,
And Fight a little longer,
Love is Out There?

ACKNOWLEDGEMENTS

I would especially like to thank Daily Mollyhorn for doing such a wonderful job on the cover artwork. I've known Daily for a few years now and I had to do a lot of begging for her personal touch. So, I would love for all you wonderful people to give Daily some 'high fives'. LOL. I'm sorry, I was just thinking…..I don't think Daily would even give someone a 'high five', but it's more for the motif of it all. My editor, Brenda Grasso, for allowing me to use all those commas. And one more, THANK YOU!

AFTERWORD

I really hope you enjoyed reading *SOOTHING MASSAGE FOR THE MIND*. It was something I really needed to do for myself, and I hope you get some insight from it. Remember this is a journey that I'm taking. I'm also bringing you beautiful people along with me. I'm not really one for long goodbyes, so until next time, wait for *SOOTHING MASSAGE FOR THE HEART*......Seeeeeeeeeeeeeeeeeeeeeeeeeeeeeeeeeeya

Douglas Alan Dodd

AFTER AFTERWORD

I have 4 *SOOTHING MASSAGE FOR THE series set to come out in the next few years. I have decided to break-up the original trilogy of books with SOOTHING MASSAGE FOR THE DEPRESSED.*

Just think of it as the biggest heartbreak you ever had, right before you found true love. I really wish I could talk more about this new edition, but you poetry junkies are gonna have to wait until May 6, 2025.

OH YEAH….there is one more thing, I have made a special Spotify, Amazon Music, and Apple Music (thanks to Amy Kyriakidis for the help) playlists to go along with this book. Just search for SOOTHING MASSAGE FOR THE MIND. Enjoy!!!

One more time,

Seeeeeeeeeeeeeeeeeeeeeeeeeeeeeeeeeeeeeeeeeya

Douglas Alan Dodd